bali houses

new wave asian architecture and design

Gianni Francione
photos by Luca Invernizzi Tettoni

PERIPLUS

Published by Periplus Editions (HK) Ltd

www.periplus.com

Copyright © 2002 Periplus Editions (HK) Ltd
Photos © 2002 Luca Invernizzi Tettoni

LCC Card No. 2004541206

ISBN: 978-0-7946-0013-6

First published, 2002

Distributors:
North America, Latin America & Europe
Tuttle Publishing, 364 Innovation Drive,
North Clarendon, VT 05759-9436 U.S.A.
Tel: 1 (802) 773-8930; Fax: 1 (802) 773-6993
info@tuttlepublishing.com
www.tuttlepublishing.com

Japan
Tuttle Publishing, Yaekari Building, 3rd Floor,
5-4-12 Osaki, Shinagawa-ku, Tokyo 141 0032
Tel: (81) 3 5437-0171; Fax: (81) 3 5437-0755
sales@tuttle.co.jp
www.tuttle.co.jp

Asia Pacific
Berkeley Books Pte Ltd.,
61 Tai Seng Avenue, #02-12
Singapore 534167
Tel (65) 6280 1330; Fax (65) 6280 6290
inquiries@periplus.com.sg
www.periplus.com

Indonesia
PT Java Books Indonesia,
Kawasan Industri Pulogadung,
Jl. Rawa Gelam IV No. 9, Jakarta 13930
Tel: (62) 21 4682-1088; Fax: (62) 21 461-0206
cs@javabooks.co.id

15 14 13 12 11   12 11 10 9 8
Printed in Singapore

Front cover and p6: Views of a cheerful
compound designed by David Lombardi.

p1: A *Rambut Sedana* statue in the
guest bedroom in Edith Jesuttis's house.

p2: Exterior view of an idyllic villa designed
by the GM architects.

p3: Wooden and metal staircase designed by
Giovanni D'Ambrosio.

This page: Looking into the guest living room
of a Japanese art lover.

Back cover: View of garden from a tropical
house by the GM architects; *nangka* wood
stools by Sumio Suzuki; corridor and open
bath area, in a quiet villa by Joost van Grieken.

Endpaper: Black resin pieces: detail on
a sushi tray by Produs Trend.

contents

Above: "Spike", a natural hardwood sculpture by Carola Vooges. *Right:* The corridor linking the dining room and the sleeping quarters in Joost van Grieken's house.

the new tropical internationalism

At the cusp of the new millennium, thousands of foreigners, many of whom are engaged in some kind of artistic activity, have made Bali their home. From Sayan to Sanur, Kintamani to Kuta, a new cosmopolitanism flourishes. This influx, from both the West and East, arrives on Bali's shores literally by the day. No longer in search of the utopian idyll as were earlier travellers, such people create a craft studio, oil an import-export business, open an artisanal workshop, and join the dream-home building boom. Feeding off the innate creativity of the Balinese and bringing new technologies and ideas from outside, they design, reinterpret and rework the much-touted concept of 'Bali style'.

Nowhere is this phenomenon more apparent than in the fields of architecture and interior design. As with their predecessors, who started coming to the island in the 1930s, these newcomers have a lifestyle that revolves around a heady combination of tropical indoor-outdoor living, island charm and artistic endeavour. But there are some significant differences in the application of their creativity—it's a case of 'Bali style' growing up, leaving home (literally as well as metaphorically) and transforming into what can be termed 'new tropical internationalism'.

Above: A large handmade glass plate sculpture by Seiki Torige. *Previous page:* The guest living room in a Japanese art lover's home looks out to a sun-dappled garden.

Yesteryear's thatched huts have become today's highly marketable garden estates. All over the island, exciting collaborations between Balinese building techniques and contemporary vision have produced new dream-homes of startling originality. Increasingly, there is a challenging dualism between tradition and modernity, organic materials and metals or plastics, high-tech components and crafted-by-hand accessories. Manual techniques of vernacular construction could sit awkwardly beside pre-fab technology, but by tapping into trends from outside rather than from within Bali, and by taking advantage of the island's plentiful

Above: Handmade glass dinner set comprising plates, glasses and candle holders by Seiki Torige. *Overleaf:* View of the swimming pool from the living area in Edith Jesuttis's Spanish-style villa.

materials, villas are created that speak volumes about the island's architectural journey. Quality is the catchword, 'Bali-based' the buzzword.

This book showcases a selection of private houses, art galleries and restaurant that best illustrates this concept of 'new tropical internationalism'. The structures certainly exist apart from—and beyond—the traditional Balinese architectural legacy, even if craft-based touches remain. There are homes with Japanese Zen influences, a restored 150-year-old Toba Batak house with a modern interior, a new villa born from Spanish colonial inspirations in the same compound as a 19th-century Joglo

Purple and cherry red tones dominate in this bedroom designed by Dean Kempnich. On the headboard is a Sumbawa stone elephant mounted on wooden base; the oil and acrylic painting is by local artist Made Kembar.

pavilion. Wooden shingles from Borneo and local *merbau* and *bengkerai* woods mix and mingle with metal, steel and plastic. Strong lines and geometric forms sometimes replace the softer *alang alang* roofs. The variety is in the architectural style; the unity comes in the fact that the buildings all somehow display a contemporary aesthetic.

None of this, of course, is entirely new. Today's designers, new-age spa operators, glass blowers and healer-potters simply represent another wave of sun-seekers in search of that elusive island magic. The intrepid travellers of the '30s found the attraction of the island then much as it is today. European artists, such as painters Walter Spies and Rudolph Bonnet, were lured by the exotic to tuck up with the Tjokorde of Ubud. They set up studio and gave birth to a creatively prolific artistic mélange of both assimilation and exchange. Others followed, primarily in the fields of painting, sculpture, dance and music.

The huge bedroom in a Japanese artist's home showcases an ancient Javanese bed, a richly coloured, patterned Indian carpet, a primitive wooden bench, and an ancestral statue from Borneo.

Later, in the '60s and '70s, another wave of often-disillusioned Westerners, this time on the hippy trail, found refuge in the island's mysticism, its peaceful Hindu population and its sarong-clad, sunny lifestyle. Many started small cottage industries—those that survived are the forebears of today's design conglomerates.

These high-flying enterprises are, for the most part, run by the most recent influx of island dwellers. They arrived on the eve of the new millennium when Bali, contrary to the rest of Indonesia, was experiencing an economic boom; true to form, they are more likely to be seen speaking urgently into a handphone than swaying somnolently on a hammock in the hills. And, of course, these movers and shakers subscribe to the tropical dream: they buy land and buy houses, start businesses, tap into the island's enduring natural and artistic resources ... and fuel the fires of commercialism. Their abilities, the island's abundance of natural materials,

Above: Laminated glass bar counter and sculpture by Seiki Torige at the Biji restaurant at Begawan Giri Estate, outside Ubud. *Right:* The living area in Mrs Sin Sin's private villa is suffused with light and space.

the flexibility of the local craftsmen who can copy-and-craft simultaneously, and the continuing growth in tourism, have spawned this next tier of talent. Today, Bali's bevy of builders, furniture designers, ceramicists, jewellery designers, fashionistas, carvers, glassmakers, lighting designers, glazers and the like, are too numerous to catalogue

In many cases, these craftsmen echo the ethos of the buildings they decorate. Carvers, furniture makers and lighting specialists often use organic materials that are plentiful in Bali: be it local wood, bone, mother-of-pearl, resin or any of the smooth stones so famed island-wide, they cut, carve, shape and coax these materials into home-makers' dreams. The designs are cutting edge, and would look as stylish in a loft in New York as on a verandah with a ricefield view. Similarly, fabrics such as *batik* and *ikat*, sourced from around the archipelago, are stamped and sewn into scatter cushions, curtains and romantic drapes for the bed. The resultant high-quality collections are now exported as well as sold within the island market. The demand for such home décor items from high-end boutiques in North America, Europe and Australia is seemingly insatiable.

Above: A table runner serves as a wall hanging and a fish lamp as a lampshade, in the Gaya Gallery, Ubud. The profile on canvas is by Filippo Sciassia. *Right:* An attractive composition of a recycled glass vessel, and two mixed media works by Seiki Torige for Esok Lusa. *Overleaf:* A bold and contemporary housing project by the GM architects.

Put simply, Bali is going global. Film-stars in Bombay commission Bali-style villas on the Indian Ocean; American television tycoons want their piece of paradise in California, Florida or the Bahamas and take their design brief from a villa complex in Bali; and private properties in Malaysia, Thailand, the Philippines, Australia and other countries in the region buy into the Bali design boom. Increasingly, Bali's villas have become the new benchmark for tropical living: their originality of expression, rising quality and intense creativity have put them centre stage in the tropical design world. Long may it continue.

colonial modern

Situated in Umalas in the Desa Bumbak region, this country residence was designed by French painter and sculptor Claude Paparella. It functions both as a private den and place of inspiration, as well as a showcase for the artist's works. The L-shaped colonial style building sits on the side of a hillock; from the garden, an interesting perspective is formed with the black terrazzo stone steps (see below left) contrasting starkly with the white *palimanan* borders as they sweep up to the back entrance of the house, meeting the verandah on the left and a covered patio on the right. In the interiors, Paparella's penchant for Zen style shows through the charming interplay between modern colonial solidity and Zen austerity.

The black and white theme reappears repeatedly in the interior design, and also in the artist's works, which are displayed throughout the house. But mediating these somber hues are the strong colours and contrasting textures in the furnishings. Various materials are used in the house—from *sirap* in the roof, coconut wood in the pillars, and white lime finish in the walls, to black cement for the flooring, *palimanan* white stone in the bathrooms, and *merbau* wood for the bedroom floors.

Opposite: The bathroom is designed in modern tropical style as an area for all purposes. As such it requires the same attention as all other living areas. In the middle of the room a brazier-like sculpture with an eye-catching red motif stands on a square of grey tiles, like a Turkish bath. Baskets of assorted sizes and textures are arranged in the back recess.

Left: The dominant colour scheme of black and white makes a striking setting in the entrance porch. The antique Javanese door and hexagonal coconut wood columns add warmth and texture. Under the white washed wooden roof, a sculpture shaped like a *chaise longue* and carved out of a single piece of teak takes pride of place. Around it are functional colonial lamps, a huge white stone vase and a contemporary painting.

27

Left: In the living room, the black and white theme is counterpointed by the contrasting pure red in the linear sofas and handmade wicker chair. This striking colour combination creates a formal yet inviting environment. In the back corner, a tall wooden table designed by the artist has Zen lines. A handmade coffee table in black, polished cement, also by Paparella, has a unique relief design; the set of funky pig carvings adds a lighter note to the whole setting.

Above: Red is once again a prominent tone in the main bedroom. The white walls and mosquito netting are a clean canvas for the old Chinese cabinet and the modern wooden sculpture. The adjoining bathroom, with its standing wash table, can be viewed through the doorway.

Left: Situated in the corner of the large and spacious living room, the lounge area is furnished with a hand-painted organza silk drape designed by Dominique Seguin, huge white floor mattresses and soft silk cushions in red, pink and lilac. This relaxing niche is well situated to catch cool cross breezes from the two large windows.

Below: The traditional setting in the smaller of two bathrooms highlights the different textures employed here. The striking black terrazzo wash basin contrasts with the white ivory stone of the standing wash table. The light coloured window drapes complete the atmosphere of luxury and privacy.

variations on a theme

Situated in the middle of rice paddies in the Kerobokan district, this project comprises three villas. Abiding by the philosophy of organic architecture, where designs are developed out of their natural surroundings, the houses showcase the spare yet dynamic spaciousness of modernist architecture. Commissioned by Mrs Sin Sin, an entrepreneur from Hong Kong, the project involved the challenge of personalizing each of the three villas while maintaining the main theme of strong and bold structural lines and planes, which is found especially in the roofs. The GM architects achieved this goal through the diversification of geometric forms, simple planes, and articulated structures that combine free-standing walls, solid, detached volumes and different levels in the flooring.

The signature of the architects—the fluidity of transition between different environments—is underscored by the use of various natural building materials and by the juxtaposition of vertical and horizontal planes. In the former, wooden shingles from Borneo are used for the roofs, and local teak and *bengkerai* are employed for the structures and interiors, while a combination of soft and hard stones is used in the walls and flooring. In the latter, an interesting composition of solids and voids is created such that a sense of unrestricted movement is achieved between the dynamic living spaces. Enhancing the feel of the continuity between inside and out is the seemingly random effect produced in the meticulously planned landscaping: paths and lawns merge, emphasizing the partnership between man and nature.

Opposite: Palimanan stone paths lead to the entrance of the living quarters, on the right, and private quarters, on the left. The wooden shingles of the bold geometric roofs are an all-embracing shelter and ease the indoor-outdoor transition. In the foreground, an ethnic stone statue welcomes guests.

Above: A modern version of the *balé* in the garden.

Left: Smooth transitions between the indoors and outdoors characterize this dining area. (See page 192 for credit details.)

Left and above: The swimming pools are a main feature of this compound. In the villa on left, the water comes right to the edge of the dining area, which is also highlighted by the striking geometric plane of the roofs that frame the house (see page 39 for a view of the interior). The view above is of another villa, and here the swimming pool laps at the sides of the living area.

Right: Geometric shapes and structures are exploited to the full in this living area; a striking sense of space and a feel of geometric majesty is created by the perfect pentagonal roof. The clean and simple design of the living area and the white background of its walls enhance the feeling of spaciousness while creating dynamic movement. Against the back of the room, a mezzanine is supported by two grey soft-stone, free-standing walls. The combination of warm wooden furniture, rich fabrics and ethnic accessories produces a subtly luxurious effect; the fusion of East and West reflects the style and taste of both the designers and the owner. The striking modern portrait and two small black and white paintings complete the finish. (See page 192 for credit details.)

Above: An all-glass ensemble of chiselled recycled glass vases, plates, and glasses handmade by Seiki Torige.

Right: In this dining room, the close relationship between the indoors and outdoors is maintained by a teak deck that opens out to and meets the swimming pool, an important design feature in the villas. The dining table contributes a minimalist feel to the room, with its sheer glass top and metal supports on chunky *paras Kerobokan* stone bases. The black modern painting on the side wall is offset by the black console table and it is an attractive contrast to the pure and clean setting of the area. (See page 192 for credit details.)

Right: Once again, here the swimming pool emphasizes the inside-outside living concept, and looks as if it is entering the deck of the dining area. The horizontal structure of the terrace above is an interesting contrast to the slope of the shingled roofs; this terrace is a good place from which to appreciate the beautiful landscaping. On right we see a modern interpretation of the traditional *balé*, a shady, open-sided area for relaxation.

Left: The detached—and seemingly suspended—roof is the defining feature of this villa, where three functional stone volumes conceal and provide access to the private quarters. The resulting convergence of strong planes, sleek lines and articulated forms creates a unique interplay of light and air. Natural materials are employed, and the combination of wood and stone with fabrics such as silk and linen contributes warmth and texture to the room. (See page 192 for credit details.)

Above: No one can resist taking a warm soak in this teak step-in Jacuzzi bath with an open view of the Japanese-style garden outside. The ethnic bamboo ladder that improvises as a towel rail is an interesting detail in this essentially spare bathroom.

Above: The clean lines of this dining area have an immediate minimalist feel, while the use of different natural materials and textures forms an effect of understated elegance. The refined ivory stone wall with inlaid wooden detail provides a fitting backdrop to the unusual coffee table, with its ancient Javanese stone support and smooth crystal glass top. The gold coloured Balinese offering and Japanese-style black pedestal with a vase on top add further interest. (See page 192 for credit details.)

Above: The stylishness of this bedroom is achieved through the tactile pleasure offered by luxurious, hand-crafted fabrics. Under the sheer airiness of the pure white mosquito net, the rich textures of the hand-printed Indian cotton bed covering, cushions, Pakistani *kilim*, and antique camel bag dominate the room, making it come alive. (See page 192 for credit details.)

Left: Wood, ivory stone and terrazzo are used for this elegant, free-standing basin fitting, a prelude to the open-air shower beyond.

in the lap of tropical luxury

Set within lush jungle in the Kenderaan village near Ubud and seated atop a steep slope, this house was developed out of its luxurious natural surroundings to serve as a private retreat, for relaxing and refuelling. The GM architects, who noted the beauty of the setting, the interest added by the hill slope, and the ancient Balinese temple on the site, decided to harness the classic tenets of organic architecture in designing the project so as to interfere as little as possible with the habitat.

Belonging to a retired Swiss businessman, the compound comprises the main building, which houses the living and dining quarters, studio mezzanine and kitchen; a separate structure for the bedrooms; and a guest house. As seen above, the main house has a clean geometric form highlighted by the low, sleek slope of the shingled roof. Its inlaid skylight of glass and wood augments the feel of the contemporary while providing ventilation upstairs and light in the living and dining areas downstairs.

The guest house (see left and overleaf), with its glass roof, is a distinctive feature built on two pyramid-like structures. The striking angularity of its walls is offset by the use of *palimanan* stone, and further enhanced by the horizontal teak inlays. Completing the jungle experience is the large, circular pool behind the main house: situated on the edge of the hill, the pool offers an excellent vantage point from which to soak in the view of the tropical surroundings.

Opposite: Located next to the sitting area, this transition area to the outdoors features an impressive huge standing lamp. As in other parts of the house, wood and glass play a key role: glass sliding doors with teak frames fill in for the walls, and the wooden frame of the roof slopes over the patio. (See page 192 for credit details.)

Below: The guest house is a striking example of what could be defined as "tropical contemporary". The building, erected on a *paras Kerobokan* stone structure, has the ivory hues of *paras Jogya* sandstone and is patterned with horizontal teak inlays. Sheltering the building is an all-embracing glass canopy with a wooden frame support. It has a two-fold purpose: it allows the sunlight to stream in while providing sufficient shade; it also keeps out the rain while allowing a view of the outside.

Right: The sitting area has an understated elegance that is set off by colourful furnishings. Simple angles and forms, and the natural surface of the wood inlay stone walls, form the backdrop for the two low 1970s German sofas, and dark finish teakwood coffee tables with bone inlay. In the corner a tall table lamp with a circular shade provides a lovely contrast to the angularity all around. The colours in the paintings by Balinese artist Wayan Karja are cleverly reproduced in the scatter cushions on the sofas. In the foreground, a pair of wooden bookends with terracotta heads are a playful touch. (See page 192 for credit details.)

Above: In the dining area, the slanted skylight, teak plank flooring, white ivory stone walls and low *paras Kerobokan* stone wall make an alluring setting of contrasting angles and geometric forms. This backdrop plays host to a sparse collection of eclectic furnishings, including a simple glass dining table accompanied by an original set of van der Mies Bauhaus chairs, and a teak wood console table in dark finish and bone inlay. Ethnic objects and modern sculptures line the sides of the room, while contemporary paintings decorate the walls. The result is a minimalist elegance, lit by the soft light filtering through the linen drapes in the skylight. (See page 192 for credit details.)

Above: Located at the back of the house, the patio cum deck in locally produced wash concrete leads to the pump house and shower room, the shady, shingled *balé* and the infinity-edge pool. A soak in the pool, which is situated at the edge of the drop-off, offers an unforgettable sensation of tranquillity and peace.

set in stone

This house perches on the steep slope of Pecatu Hill in Uluwatu, overlooking the countryside and the Indian Ocean. These views are particularly breathtaking from the roof-top swimming pool (see above). When Italian architect and designer Giuseppe Verdacchi came upon this unique place, he immediately saw the significance not only of the location but also the site: this was an old limestone quarry that had been extracted for centuries by the locals. The traditional method of cutting the stone with saws and chisels had left beautiful intricate geometric patterns on the rock face; these now form part of the backdrop of the house. The objectives of the whole architectural project were to preserve the original strong character of the site as well as to integrate the new building into the environment such that the house became almost invisible from below.

The interiors were designed around the bold beauty of the back limestone walls. In the spacious living area, there are striking contrasts of perspectives, shapes and materials. A medley of different textures in the bathrooms blends well together to bring about smooth, cool fusion. Elsewhere, the skilful mix and match of natural woods, stone and antique pieces bring about a sense of elegant abundance. Overall, this is an environment in which no detail is overlooked.

Opposite: The rectangular shapes of wooden tabletop and lava stone supports and the high-backed chairs are particularly grounding in this cool, airy and luminous verandah. The elegant sobriety of the furnishings and decorative elements are skilfully complemented by the colour scheme of black, brown, grey and ivory.

Left: This relaxation area is set against white *palimanan* flooring and features an adjustable sofa with royal blue upholstery, designed and handmade by the architect, and an old Dutch fridge and travel trunk used as a coffee table.

Left: The marble-like quality of limestone—its strength, porosity and translucence—forms the unique beauty of the back walls in the living area. Here the original limestone rock face has been skillfully hewn polished, and highlighting its texture are the natural light and a small waterfall. The effect is intriguing as the outside becomes a part of the inside. The architectural design within is simple: the dark wood used in the roof and ivory stone in the flooring provide a classic setting. An imposing central ivory stone column reinforces the strong character of the room, while also grounding the eloquent furnishings—made of black lava stone and teak—and fascinating accessories. Most of the furniture pieces and decorative objects have been custom designed by Verdacchi himself, and artfully arranged to set off the intrinsic intensity of the place.

Above: Each of the areas in the house has been designed with an atmosphere that befits its distinctive purpose. Here in the bedroom, the use of natural wood and cozy colours provides a warm and comfortable feeling, while the collection of antique items, such as the old Javanese doors and set of Dutch colonial suitcases, gives a timeless reassurance. In the background are modern custom-built wardrobe units. The only bold details, common to the rest of the house, are the lava stone supports for the king-sized bed.

Above: The classical feel of this bathroom is achieved by the sheer boldness and beauty of the original rock, which has been hand-carved into simple planes. Reminiscent of a Roman spa, the bath is designed for Spartan but sensuous bathing. Wooden columns, warm tiled flooring and tropical plants highlight the pleasurable purposefulness of the surroundings.

Left: The natural hues of ivory stone in this walk-in bathroom complement the bold supports of the basin and mirror fitting. These supports were roughly hewn from a piece of limestone rock—which stands where it was originally found—and polished to become as translucent as marble. Two wooden pillars frame the fitting; antique Dutch colonial bottles provide luminous contrast. A step-in bath is filled with colourful flowers.

Opposite: This open bathroom is constructed on different levels and shows the designer's talent for mixing and matching textural opposites as well as striking shapes and colours. The warm tones of the inlaid floor tiles create geometrical symmetry. The attractive corner washstand, framed by two stand-alone teak bathroom cabinets—hand-crafted by the architect provide pleasing functional detail. The tactile magnetism of the rough quarry rock contrasts dramatically with the refined finishes of the furnishings, resulting in a pleasantly bold and inviting effect. For a view of the bath area, see page 57.

spanish delight in bali

This house in Legian was designed and furnished by owner Edith Jesuttis, an Austrian fashion designer who has lived and worked in Bali for twelve years. When designing the house, Jesuttis had in mind the Spanish colonial house, with the customary patio at its heart. The building is constructed in a U-shape, which embraces a patio. A detached pavilion located just beyond the waterfall, the Joglo House, closes the 'U'.

From without, the house looks—and is—compact, but within the design reveals a modern exploitation of space. The curve of the "sunset bridge" at the entrance to the compound (see below left) is an interesting contrast against the taller angularity of the house. At the main entrance, the sound of gently cascading water teasingly beckons one to the patio, and it is at this open area that one feels a strong sensation of having reached an oasis of peace and privacy.

The main feature of the patio is a long swimming pool made from green unpolished stone and flanked by bottle palm trees. Beyond the pool, the Joglo house stands in full splendour: this was a 19th-century royal pavilion from Madura, now transformed into a luxurious guest house. Certainly, the feel in the airy living areas is one of comfort and ease, but the private niches, beautiful patio and quaint pavilion in the garden also hearken to the old Moorish legacy, and have an Arabian Nights quality about them.

Opposite: Standing in conspicuous isolation at a corner of the dining room, a long single-block teak dining table, with Timorese motifs along its sides, dominates the area. Its two supports are anchored by a long horizontal base—a modern touch. On the wall in the background is a traditional Irian Jaya painting on bark.

Above: A *Rambut Sedana* statue representing Dewa Vishnu.

Above: The T-shaped swimming pool—the main focus of the patio—is designed to face West so that the beauty of the Balinese sunset can be fully savoured. Here at the heart of the house, the feeling of having arrived at a private oasis is enhanced by the choice of colours and natural materials. The colour of the palm fronds is reflected in the green of the pool, and the natural tones of pebbles, white ivory stone, and pebble-wash white finish of the sunset bridge complement the warm *bengkerai* wood in the flooring perfectly.

Opposite: The master bedroom has the same feel of intimate seclusion as the lounge in the main house. Elegant silk mosquito nets softly frame the coconut wood bed, harmonizing with the rich teak of the flooring and the warm tones of the precious Afghanistan rug. Two royal *cili* statues symbolizing Dewi Sri, goddess of rice and prosperity, silently stand watch.

Overleaf: The living room, located at the end of the swimming pool, extends the sense of space and light that characterizes the house. Set on a *palimanan* stone floor, the furnishings include two rattan sofas with fitted cushioning in black linen, white silk pillows, and a glass-topped table crafted from an Irian Jaya canoe. On the latter, a white stone horse and rider carving from Sumba is displayed.

Left: The décor in this secluded corner of the small lounge in the main house is reminiscent of the Arabian Nights—it appears to have been designed for the exchange of intimacies and confidences and private story-telling sessions *à la* Scheherazade. Silk curtains gracefully drape the large ivory terrazzo sofa base, and a plush red silk mattress and cushions provide comfort and warmth. An old Balinese painting "*Ider Ider*" depicts the Hindu god Arjuna being distracted by angels while meditating. In the wall niches, two ornate boxes with secret compartments in the back, store *lontars* (ancient Balinese scripts on leaves), recording clan histories. A sinuous statue of a female figure representing Dewi Sri, goddess of rice and prosperity, is mounted on the wall. Called *Rambut Sedana,* this type of statue is fashioned almost entirely from old Chinese coins, except for the head, hands and feet, which are made of wood and covered with gold leaf.

Above: White *palimanan* stone floors, pebble wash finishing for the walls, and *alang alang* in the ceiling set the scene for the bathroom, which combines the comfort of traditional facilities with the pleasures of open-air bathing. Warm teak is used in the wash table, which is decorated with an inlaid shell motif, while soft lighting illuminates the functional wall niches fitted with mirrors.

Below and left: The 19th-century royal pavilion from Madura houses a guest room, which exudes comfort and tranquillity. Inside, fine ceiling-to-floor mosquito nets frame the beds, setting off the rich colour of the handwoven silk bedspread with antique Laotian decorations, while the old Pakistani carpet adds tactile interest. The focal point of the room, however, is the lamp base, which is in the form of Sendi, or "The Lady with Wings", a Balinese symbol of prosperity. The statue-lamp is set at the head of the bed and blesses the room and its occupants.

a quiet haven

Located along the Wos River valley five kilometres (three miles) north of Ubud, this villa was designed by Dutch architect Joost van Grieken as a place for quiet relaxation and for entertaining friends. This restful effect is made possible through careful synthesis of the characteristics of the exterior with the interior design. The former shows solidity and strength, and is in harmony with the surroundings, while the latter presents simple functional forms, sensual colours and a selection of traditional handicrafts.

By using a limited selection of materials Joost enhances the simplicity and purity of the house. Lombok grasses form the thatch for the roof, but *bengkerai* wood is used in the roof framework, as well as for all door and window fittings, and the octagonal load-bearing columns; the latter are supported by bases of resilient Javanese white stone. In addition, custom made ivory and polished cement tiles make elegant statements in all pavilions, while the walls are either finished in cream-coloured Javanese sandstone or plastered and painted in Canton green or Tuscan terracotta.

There are several good places in the compound for resting, talking and savouring nature. The spacious, clean-lined dining area is perfect for chatting. The lounge directly across from here offers the best views over the garden and valley. A long corridor (see opposite) linking the service areas to the sleeping quarters also leads one to the west-facing sitting area, where the beauty of the sunset or moonrise can be enjoyed over a leisurely drink.

Above: Rectangular white stone slabs form a bridge between the dining room and the lounge area.

Left: At the entrance of the house, this modern interpretation of the traditional *aling aling* greets the visitor.

Opposite: Clean lines and pure geometry characterize this outdoor staircase, which leads to the roof of the house. Two Garuda statues safeguard the passage of those who venture upstairs for a view of the valley.

Above: Under a traditional thatched roof in the dining area, a table in the form of a block of solid teak is supported by two symmetrically placed rectangular columns of *wonosobo* ivory stone. The free-standing sandstone wall conceals the long corridor that links this room to the back gallery and private areas.

Right: Situated between the living quarters and the bedrooms, this west-facing sitting area is furnished with a daybed set on dark wooden blocks—perfect for reclining on.

Above: Shapes, colours and materials in a Canton green palette dominate this bedroom where traditional and modern elements are combined. The curve of the free-standing wall in the corner contrasts with the linear purity of the black wooden base of the square bed. This wall not only screens a private dressing room but also gives access to the bathroom behind (see opposite). Arranged on the terrazzo ledge of the fixed headboard are old Javanese bedpost pieces, Kalimantan weaving, and candle holders, while a set of Indian travel boxes at the side add a feeling of timelessness and repose to the room.

Opposite: The perfect oval of the terrazzo green bathtub is backed by a vibrant Canton green wall, while the natural tone of the Jogyakarta stone side walls, the ivory stone slabs and white river stone floor set the mood for open air bathing. A brown Chinese vase with a tropical plant adds interest.

Left: Despite the simple furnishings, a modish touch is found in this bedroom. The royal blue fabric of the bed covering, alongside the vibrant red of the cushions and runner, is offset by natural tones of the sandstone wall. Ethnic wall hangings and Irian Jaya artefacts complete the picture.

Left: In this open patio bathroom, the warm Tuscan terracotta painted wall, rectangular shower fitting, and oval terrazzo tub on pebbles and sandstone slabs make a very pleasing picture. Two rattan woven baskets complete this well balanced composition of geometrical shapes.

Above: The pure round shape of the basin interacts with the angular forms of the sculpture-like wash table. Green terrazzo and black details pleasantly contrast with the ivory hues of the back wall.

79

timeless splendour

Located in the Canggu district, this property comprises a L-shaped main house with a large garden and a detached guest villa. It belongs to a Japanese art lover. The main entrance is characterized by a thatched roof and a free standing wall constructed of *batu putih*, a local soft white limestone (see below left). The simple façade belies the planning that has gone into the design of the entire compound, making it a remarkable showcase not only of the art pieces, but also of the owner's gift of synthesizing old with modern. The grass lawn around the house, for one, has been carefully cultivated, and huge palm trees produce an intriguing play of light and shadows (see above).

Inside the house, the owner's love of timeless art is paramount. An immense feeling of space and freedom pervades throughout; permitting this are the expanses of white plastered walls and the large, white square tiles of polished cement—evidence again of careful forethought. Unfettered by superfluous decorative detail, the one-off furniture pieces and art objects—primitive art, inorganic sculptures, contemporary paintings, colonial accessories, or modern detail—speak for, and among, themselves. Notwithstanding the art gallery effect, this house also has a homely touch, and is a comfortable place in which to live, relax and savour art.

Left: The rustic main entrance to the compound belies the enormous talent showcased within.

Opposite: Paved in white *palimanan* stone, the patio displays art works in natural forms by local artists. The chair sculpture and obelisk are each worked from a single piece of teak. In the foreground is a modern roughly-cut blue glass dish by Seiki Torige.

Previous page (see also pages 4, 10): The guest living room is characterized by white walls and floors, and natural tones and materials. The rattan sofa, furnished with soft silk cushions, is complemented by a low table made out of a light sheet of teak; old chairs, ancient statues, a Bornean mat, and a contemporary painting bond to make up the rest of this 'living' art gallery. A wide, open entrance to the garden contributes to the sense of freedom and space.

Above: The entrance courtyard has a Zen-like sobriety, with pale mottled *paras* walls counteracting the regular black volcanic stone floor. The door, which is made of two weathered panels of teak, has an unexpected touch of modernity in the form of an unusual handle, made out of a piece of melted aluminium.

Right: The spacious and luminous main living room, with its white walls and flooring, stages a breathtaking fusion of ancient and modern art. In the middle of the room is a low table—actually a large panel of black *kafini* forest wood resting on four carved antique pedestals. Arranged around it are a Dutch colonial daybed (in the foreground), a couch carved from one single block of teak, and an antique Javanese bench (partially shown). Next to the ancient teak doors, a small table with streamlined tubular stainless steel legs supports an ancient stone sculpture, while a contemporary mixed media painting graces the back wall.

Above: The entrance from the garden courtyard leads to this inner hallway, an 'exhibit space' where ethnic fuses with modern-chic, simplicity with richness, against a backdrop of candid white walls and a terracotta floor. The painting on the back wall is flanked by an ancient Bornean statue of welcome and a large white stone, once a rudimentary grindstone. Facing each other across a low wood table are two primitive rustic chairs. An antique door panel from Timor with a fertility symbol carved on it is on the left.

Opposite: In this corner of the main living room, the white expanse of the walls and flooring are a perfect backdrop for the honeyed, mellow tone and tactile beauty of natural teak. Supported by two ivory pedestals, the 'wall unit' is a contemporary show-case for two pieces of primitive art, which flank a contemporary painting. In the foreground a slim sheet of teak rests on contrasting stainless steel supports on an old Bornean mat.

Overleaf: The guest bedroom, discreetly set apart from the main house, offers the same feel of boundless space and light as the other living areas. Here, a typical Chinese style bed unit is furnished with a slim mattress and soft hangings of natural fabric, silk cushions and lamp. Complementing the bed are a dark wood colonial table, an old, oriental lounge chair and a primitive stool. Completing the composition are the square form of a rich red carpet and a contemporary painting.

Left: A sleek lawn and the sinuous majesty of palm trees produce amazing light and shadow effects, an unusual yet ideal garden setting for an art collection. In the foreground is a huge, time-worn vat in soft stone, once used for the traditional dyeing of textiles, now a captivating water garden.

Left and below: The garden setting is perfect for the collection of unusual, ancient wood and stone artworks, which seem so well ensconced they appear to spring, uncannily, from nature itself. The sense of space and light appears to develop as one continues to observe the scene, such that the aged artworks curiously evolve into pure abstract art to become examples of the ultra modern: they belong to the present time.

the persistence of memory

Located in Pantai Brawa in the Canggu area, this two-storey house was constructed entirely out of old teakwood and set in the middle of rice fields. The owner, Aulia, originally from Sumatra, Indonesia, has lived in Bali for more than twenty years and he designed this place.

As he loves vernacular Indonesian art and enjoys being surrounded by quality works, Aulia fills the rustic interiors as well as the compound with creative art pieces collected from throughout the country. One example is the ancient millstone (see above), which is reminiscent of the day-to-day village life that existed before the advent of industry. These primitive artworks not only inspire with their antiquity, but they also make a point about the cyclical and continuous nature of life. The reality of the past thus co-exists with a present interpretation of it in a seamless marriage of traditional and contemporary.

The tone is set at the entrance to the compound (see left), as an ancient panel supported by primitive pillars, together with a tree sculpture, greets the visitor. A simple wooden fence running along the border of the premises leads one further into the intriguing compound. Further on, one finds the entrance doorway in a very modern stone and wood design, beyond which an old Sumba stone acts as an *aling aling* (see overleaf). Protecting yet inviting, this screen offers an ideal setting for the works of primitive art skilfully arranged within.

Opposite: From the main house one has an overview of the compound—and of the originality and creativity of the owner. Attracting attention is the unusual shape of the lily pond: its borders are lined with ancient stone troughs, which were used for drinking and washing. Primitive sculptures are placed as if at random around the compound, co-existing with the outhouses and the natural vegetative setting.

Below: An ancient Osa-Osa stone seat from Nias island (in the foreground) and a series of squared teakwood posts comprise a contemporary still life composition.

Bottom: At the entrance to the house, an old teakwood door framed by natural-cut green stones greets the guest. The picture on right shows the old Sumba stone *aling aling* on the other side of the door.

Right: This open sided wide space functions as both the living and dining areas. Set on the dining table in the foreground is a contemporary handmade ceramic dinner set from Jenggala Keramik; it adds a touch of sophistication to the otherwise rustic ambience. (See also page 96.)

Opposite: The spacious backdrop of this living and dining area comprises wood panelling, traditional rafters, square pillars and a simple staircase, which allows primitive wood and stone artworks to take pride of place. In the foreground is a huge one-piece teakwood table top on wooden blocks.

Above: The owner's uncanny ability to integrate past and present is staged at the entrance courtyard. Seen here is the stone and wood doorway whose contemporary frame contrasts with that of the large *kulkul*, or traditional tubular wooden drum, and a *tau tau* effigy on a rustic chair.

Above: A perfect symphony of solid shapes and old precious woods achieve a surprisingly post-modern feel in the bedroom; an ancient wooden panel and a traditional fabric hanging only add to the effect.

Opposite: The primary textures of stone and wood, coupled with the simple lines of an old wooden pillar and stone water jar, achieve an exquisite and quintessentially Zen feel in this traditional Bali washroom.

a funky abode

A designer who has worked in places as far afield as Japan, Canada and Europe, David Lombardi enjoys creating "funky" houses. His home in Canggu is one opportunity that has allowed his creative streak full expression. Surrounded by rice paddies and pandan fields, the house immediately gives one the impression of playful irreverence. The juxtaposition of contrasting shapes and volumes, and of different textures, materials and primary colours, adds interest and unexpected detail to all living spaces, giving them a refreshing and fun effect.

The whole compound develops through a single axis to embrace all—the entrance, buildings, pool and landscaping. From the entrance, a walkway leads to a transitional living area, whose traditional *alang alang* structure clad in bamboo half conceals and half highlights a modern blue building, and creates a visual tunnel that encourages one to enter. This distinctive structure houses the kitchen in its left wing and a suspended office in its right.

Beyond this transition, a whole visual treat beckons (see front cover of book): the rice paddies and terraced garden, itself a paddy, a long swimming pool, and several cabanas sharing an undulating *alang alang* roof. At the end of the pool, a bridge takes one over to the family private quarters, where the lounge area, dining room and bedrooms are located, overlooking the open-air breakfast patio and *balé*. From this part of the compound (see opposite), one can literally look back on the cohesiveness of the design. Despite the unusual features, the amalgamation of the various geometric shapes and volumes, the choice of material and the contrasting colours combine to produce a synergistic whole in a wonderful natural setting.

Left: A free-standing partition wall in a bedroom, separating the bed from the walk-in wardrobe.

Above: A still-life composition of stone and organic material, set in a niche near the breakfast patio.

Right: The ivory slabs of the walkway leads one from the entrance (see above) to the transitional living area—a tall structure with an *alang alang* thatched roof that stands out against the sharp contrast of the blue building housing the kitchen and office.

Above: Forming the entrance to the house is a traditional thatched roof over a black wooden door set in an ivory stone frame, and a simple bamboo fence. Balancing natural tone and organic materials with contrasting shapes, the overall form is welcoming.

Left (see also front cover): On the other side of the transitional living area, one is greeted by a clean rectangular swimming pool, flanked by verdant rice paddies and cabanas, and framed by the family private quarters.

Below: Funky and functional—surrounding the entire dining area on the first floor of the family quarters, these slumped glass panels are by Seiki Torige.

Above: Housed on the long side of the L-shaped living area, the dining room has an enviable view of the surrounding pandan fields and rice paddy of the garden. The refreshing atmosphere in the dining area is subtly achieved through the playful contrast of materials, textures and colour tones. The lighter-coloured slanted posts vie for attention against the darker main frame of the roof, while the recycled-glass tabletop and tableware are elegantly matched with the dark wood of the seats, of the long wooden storage units lining the outer length, and of the rectangular cupboard at the end of the table.

Opposite: The beautiful outdoor patio just outside the private quarters is an ideal place for taking breakfast and savouring the splendour of morning. Against the clean white tiles of the flooring, the bright blue of the breakfast counter stands out in playful contrast to the red painted square frame of the exit. A vernacular note is offered by the thatched *balé* with a raised wooden deck, which provides a sheltered space for relaxing. Once again we find an unexpected element—an old Sumba stone standing on the border of the patio, like a directional signpost.

Above: Just across the bridge from the swimming pool, the lounge area has a playful feel about it, contributed in part by the slanted light-coloured posts. Primary colour returns in the red of the cushions on the sofa and easy chair, while the light colour of the latter and of the planked flooring is set off by the dark of the solid wood coffee table on an old mat from Borneo.

Above: This bathroom, while embracing the Balinese trend of open air bathing, is fashioned around the concept of the Japanese tea room and garden with a *koi* pond. The usual Japanese sobriety is enlivened by the introduction of refreshing primary colours: red in the walls and blue in the wash table.

Left: A modern table lamp in undulating perforated metal design, by Esok Lusa, on a dark wooden storage unit.

a batak legacy

Belonging to Austrian Edith Jesuttis, this 150-year-old Toba Batak house has a carved and painted façade that features four *singa*. According to an ancient Batak legend, this mythological creature represents the Boru Saniang Naga, or the snake-god that carried the world.

Originally located in the middle of Lake Toba in North Sumatra, Indonesia, the rectangular, wooden structure was later transported to Bali. The original design of the house was preserved during the reconstruction, and the building is now firmly ensconced in a jungle in Baturiti, near Bedugul. Its tall, sharply sloping thatched saddle roof with outward leaning gables (above) resembles a ship—a traditional Toba Batak architectural design. The roof rises above its tropical environment, both dominating it as well as blending into it.

Traditionally, Toba Batak houses comprised three levels: an unwalled basement for housing livestock, the ground floor for the family members, and an attic for storing provisions and valuable objects. The restoration works did away with the basement, and one now finds the dining room, bathroom, kitchen and sauna on the ground level, and the sleeping and living area under the high saddle roof. The project is a fascinating example of how a traditional dwelling can be adapted to a contemporary lifestyle— a successful reworking of a timeless classic.

Left: Along the entrance corridor are two antique Lombok drums and a painting by Balinese artist Salim.

Opposite: Skillfully exploiting the form of the high roof, Jesuttis arranged rich and colourful organza and raw silk drapes to gently frame the sitting and sleeping room. A 65-year-old carpet from Uzbekistan, a teakwood opium table, Indian silver-based lamps and an old wrought iron chandelier complete the sumptuous look. (See page 192 for credit details.)

Left: Surrounded by lush vegetation, a circular wooden staircase leads one from the carpark to the house. The lily pond at its base functions as the ideal transition between the outdoors and indoors, and a night flame blazes after dusk to illuminate the way. White paving stones and pebbles lay the passageway from indoors to out.

Above: The dark ironwood used for the posts, slatted walls, and floors recreate an old Japanese feel, complementing the original decorated panels above.

Above: A rustic wooden bathtub, a bamboo water pipe, and an old glazed water jar form a romantic alfresco tropical bath setting at the back of house.

Left: No respectable Balinese dwelling will do without a *balé*. Designed for open-air relaxation, the modern *balé* enjoys a wide variety of interpretations. Here we have the rich tones of iron-wood, coupled with decorating panels and sumptuous silks.

Above and left: Two views of the garden, which comes complete with a *balé* and a pool, set on an ironwood floor.

nomadic chic

Situated on the edge of the Campuhan River in Payogan, Ubud, Anneke van Waesberghe's house embraces what she calls a "nomadic chic" lifestyle. It is a place in which visitors can find peace and quiet, and a welcome respite from the hustle and bustle of their travels. Indeed, "*payogan*" means "a place for yoga" in Balinese, and perhaps it is this meaning that has inspired her in the interior design.

As rest and relaxation are a priority, furnishings throughout the house have been chosen to ensure maximum flexibility and minimum fuss. Luxury is subtly hinted at in the sumptuous textures of the natural coloured fabrics, and in the rustic finishes of the woods, hewn in basic shapes and forms. A corner of the living room (see below left) epitomizes the subtle, discreet elegance achieved throughout the house.

From the house, the sweeping views of the river valley and of the jungle and mountains beyond instill an immense sense of peace and oneness. The restful scenery and the soothing, elegant interior décor come together to comprise the haven that Anneke envisioned. It is the perfect place in which to host and pamper friends.

Above: Pillows on a daybed, showing original pillowcase designs by the owner.

Opposite: Located on the second floor, these open bedrooms are segregated only by lofty voile curtains and mosquito nets. The choice of natural finishes of wood and plain textiles provides the ideal backdrop for the surroundings beyond. Beneath the height of the roof, one can imagine sleeping out in the open, under the stars. During the day, the beds are used as couches, hence extending the living space.

Opposite: Nature dominates in the living room; the leitmotif is green, played in the walls, the fabric of the pillowcases and cushions, and the nature-themed art pieces in the wall niches. The centrepiece low table reflects the rustic textural quality that characterizes the entire interiors. On the back wall, a traditional rice paddy hat is used as a lampshade, while two carved wood artworks from Sumba and Java stand out against the pale backdrop.

Above: A contemporary still-life in a corner of the living room: Against a plain white backdrop, simple elements in the form of glass and etched stone become an altar-like console, upon which local hand-crafted objects are displayed.

Above: Micky the cat seems to enjoy lounging on the bed, made up with white linen and voile curtains, in this airy bedroom on the second storey. A tropical hat from Vietnam and a lacquered thermos from Burma stand on a leather and black canvas suitcase, set next to the bed.

Above: A restful sitting area on the ground floor that opens out to the garden is protected from the glare of the midday sun by voile and silk curtains. The large daybed is arranged in a comfortable quasi-Janus sofa, decked with pillows and bolsters.

Above: In this romantic and cosy bedroom laid with large white-dyed wooden floor planks, a Chinese-style bamboo bed with snow-white bedcover is cocooned by a mosquito net. A light canvas curtain functions as a partition between the sleeping and the working areas. The desk, in colonial Javanese style, overlooks the rice paddies and has a good sunset view.

Above: Two cabana-style portable cabinets of white canvas, located in an upstairs bedroom, offer efficient storage systems for categorizing clothing, shoes and accessories.

a bold approach

Situated in the Kerobokan region, this two-storey abode belongs to the Greek Bournias family. Designed by Italian architect Giovanni D'Ambrosio, the unconventional project suits the hot and humid Indonesian climate, and is a good example of modern tropical architecture. The design of the house is characterized by bold minimalism and contemporary linearity, and this is immediately evident from the entrance of the house (see below left). Here, the sloping roof rests on a square framework, and a wooden louvered canopy provides shade.

In the interiors, there is a functional yet aesthetically pleasing 'walk-through' effect, which comes from the skilful moulding of the spaces, and the form of the roof. The latter is a sheet metal sloping structure that leaves the house open on all sides. About one metre thick, this roof has a two-fold purpose: the corrugated metal surface provides protection from the elements, while the space between the roof and its wooden under panelling keeps the house cool via cross ventilation.

Above: A close-up of the dining table designed by D'Ambrosio: Small leaf-shaped pieces of brass wedged between two sheets of glass create the illusion of golden leaves scattered by the wind.

Left: At the entrance to the house, the angular wooden deck and the incline of the stairway that leads to the top floor create a striking impact.

Opposite: The view from the garden at the back of the house. The bed of black pebbles, the heavy-set sculpture-like stone walls, and the louvered canopy of the roof come together to form an impression of installation art.

Opposite: The décor of the dining area is bold in its contrast of materials and colours. (See page 192 for credit details.)

Right: The striking, minimalist character of the supporting structure is enhanced by the use of glass and wood in the living area; the frames of the large doors add a contemporary feel, as do the divan and standing lamp. (See page 192 for credit details.)

Above: In the master bedroom, captivating contrast is achieved between the dark tones of the wood flooring and slate stone walls, and the crimson finish in one wall and the bed head. A walk-in en suite bathroom is located in the back raised area. A modern bamboo standing lamp completes the décor. (See page 192 for credit details.)

a tropical mountain retreat

Christopher Noto, an American art and antiques dealer based in Singapore, owns Villa Uma, the house of his dreams. Designed as a luxurious, private tropical retreat in Ubud, the villa boasts an enviable location—a ridge high in the mountain jungle. With no way through to the other side of the gorge and the only access along a narrow 100-yard (90-metre) path through rice fields (see above), solitude is guaranteed. From the house, the tropical scenery stretches as far as the eye can see.

Designed in the modern tradition of American rationalism, the house, with its geometrical simplicity and spare use of ornamentation, is set among such abundant foliage that it could almost be called a modern tree house. Emphasis is on inside-outside living where the transition from the lounge and dining areas, to the deck and swimming pool, and to the tropical wilderness beyond are seamless and natural. The bedrooms, too, have been built to capture the same natural ethos, so the en suite facilities include, unsurprisingly, open-air baths. The overall feeling is of peace and connection with the environment.

Left: The exterior and deck of the house.

Opposite: An ethnic-eclectic feeling characterizes the upstairs living area. Arranged around a wooden "new art deco" coffee table are a colonial Javanese bench, a sculpture-like standing lamp, made out of one piece of coconut tree trunk, and a simple '70s teakwood cabinet. An ancient wooden grind-wheel mounted on the wall, a dried coconut leaf on the cabinet, and an 18th-century Burmese bronze on the coffee table complete the décor.

Opposite: Pure bliss—the emerald-tiled rectangular pool, with its open wooden deck, nestles amid the dense tropical foliage.

Above: From an unusual flat-roofed *balé* at the entrance to the compound, one enjoys a wide-angle view of the swimming pool and the luxuriant valley beyond.

Left: The outdoor dining area also offers an uninterrupted view of the tropical valley scenery.

Opposite: In the indoor dining area, an oversized mirror framed in dark stained ironwood rests on a solid teakwood console with dark coconut-trunk legs. On the right a standing coconut trunk sculpture completes the strong trendy-ethnic composition.

Above: A pleasantly patterned partition in teak and mirror, located inside the many niches, functions as a headboard in the second-storey master bedroom. The two standing lamps, designed by Jaya Ibrahim, together with the rattan *chaise* and ottoman, add an art deco accent.

fluid transitions

The constant quest of the GM architects is to achieve true symbiosis between architecture and the natural environment, such that the former is interpreted as developing from its immediate surroundings. A recent accomplishment, this house is an excellent example of the architects' style. The modern design is evident in the sloping planes of the roofs (see above), which form the protective shelters of the intriguing open-sided villa.

As the dominant theme in this house is nature, water plays a vital role in its design. Thus the free-form pool (see below left), situated between the living area and the garden, subtly defines the boundaries between the two areas, while maintaining the outside-inside feel of modern tropical living.

Reinforcing the close relation between building and nature is the exploitation of local stones, carefully selected for their tactile qualities and soft, delicate tones. The external and internal walls of grey and pink blend well with the Cirebon ivory stone used in most of the flooring. Despite the very modern form of the house, the effect is peaceful and tranquil; nothing is out of place or looks contrived.

Opposite: Warmth, light, and freedom characterize this spacious living area. The striking volume created by the gently sloping wooden roof structure forms a perfect interim between the house and nature outside. Equally reassuring are the natural wood tones of the roof, as well as the colour scheme—golds with natural whites and creams—and the choice of fabrics—rich materials such as cotton and silk. In the foreground an ebony black *kafini* coffee table displays a shaped 'pie' unit in palm tree wood. (See page 192 for credit details.)

Above: A waterfall gently tumbles into a lily pond as roughly hewn stepping stones guide one to the entrance of the house. There is a Zen-like quality about this contemporary entrance, enhanced by the pure geometry of planes and volumes. The delicate hues of pink and light grey stone walls, are subtly complemented by the white pebbles.

Right: The living area looks out to the garden, which reveals an idyllic combination of natural elements—water, stone and luxuriant green foliage. A white stone pathway, interjected by huge slabs of roughly hewn stone, leads one over a manicured lawn and round the curve of the free form swimming pool. The local green stone used for the undulating back wall complements the natural setting, and backs a dressed traditional Balinese altar.

Left: Light filters through cotton drapes to illuminate the dining area, which is located under a glazed open verandah. The shaped 'pie' unit and the top of the dining table are finely worked from palm tree wood. In the foreground on the left, an oversized dried coconut leaf sculpture stands on a stone base. Dark and light tones deeply interplay to create a quality ambience. (See page 192 for credit details.)

Below: A modern yet cosy feeling greets one in this elaborately designed bathroom, in which a combination of orange-ivory tones of the walls, floors and basins are complemented by the warm presence of teakwood.

living with nature

Viewed from the pool, this house, beautifully framed by white frangipani and red coral trees (see above), is another example of contemporary architecture in present-day Bali designed by the GM architects. The main volume is defined by two layers of overlapping shingled roofs. Gently sloping towards—and almost touching—the garden, they provide protection from the elements while creating wide spaces inside, where the use of natural woods and stone creates a feeling of tranquillity and harmony. From the living area, one looks out to an idyllic garden (see below left), which stages a beautiful collection of antique wood and stone objects.

The secret to the spare, contemporary beauty of the interiors is not immediately obvious, as the furnishings, when considered individually, are simple to the point of being plain. However, the overall atmosphere is one of subtle luxury, achieved through the clever exploitation of volumes, shapes and materials.

The roof is set at several angles, and this variance is complemented in various ways, such as by the use of steps, and the introduction of a mezzanine in the living room. The mixture of smooth and rough surfaces and finishes also contributes to the effect. The result is a showcase of modern living in which the emphasis is on space and light, texture and quality.

Opposite: **This entrance captures the very essence of a house in which man's need for protection from the elements is in perfect symbiosis with nature. The rich ironwood roofing provides all the comforting reassurance of shelter while the paving of white stone slabs and a pebble walk achieve the natural transition from outside to the inside. The whole feel of the setting is further highlighted by the reflection of the lily pond against the back wall and the traditional Saraswati sculpture of protection.**

Above: The skilful management of volumes and space transforms this simple sky-lighted corridor to the sleeping quarters and the detached master bedroom into an attractive area, which reflects the same contemporary elegance achieved throughout the house. The functional in-built teak display unit presents a collection of wood and stone fossils, which contrasts with the modern linear form of the standing lamp, designed by Marc Le.

Opposite: Set on an elegant pebble-washed floor in this dining room is a massive dining table resting on equally imposing trunks of black wood. Its size is offset by the warm wood tones, and its form is complemented by that of the dining chairs in teak and rattan. A modern glass and wood standing lamp by Marc Le blends in well to this contemporary environment well, completing the subtle elegance.

Right: In the living area, the contemporary design of the stone slab of the coffee table resting on two smooth wooden supports; the interesting detail of the lamp stands formed from ancient stone pillar capitals from Java; and the visual impact achieved by two finely-decorated Batak support columns on a smooth ivory stone base, from Sumatra, are examples of how contrasts in shapes, materials and age can be blended to bring about a clean, modern look.

interior reflections

The Nero Bali restaurant, located in the heart of the Legian district, was designed by Italian architect Giovanni D'Ambrosio. Using only low-cost and basic industrial materials, such as pre-cast corrugated cement slabs, small blocks of wood and sheets of mirrors, D'Ambrosio concocted a 'recipe' that entailed the "re-interpretation of the use and employment of forms and materials in everyday supply". All of these humble ingredients have been carefully and creatively integrated into the design of the place.

The focal point of the Nero Bali is the stairway, which leads to the upper dining floor. The stairs are entirely flanked on both sides by mirrors, an ingenious device meant not only to conceal the kitchen underneath, but also to create an amazing visual treat as multi-reflections of the surroundings are continuously formed as one moves through the restaurant.

The materials selected for the perimeter and other walls have equally striking results (see opposite): the white pre-cast cement slabs, with their strong texture and an almost bas-relief effect, contrast dramatically with solid dark wood blocks or black stones in rustic finish. On the second floor, simple wooden crates form decorative standing lamp pillars (see above) adding a functional yet avant-garde feel to the place. The result—a chic and trendy restaurant—is dazzling.

Left: No detail, no matter how small, has been left to chance. D'Ambrosio, who designed all the fittings, combines striking finishes with functional inventiveness. On the first floor, tables are simple, clean planes supported on tripods, from which one of the supports is elongated to become a bracket for a charming fairy light.

Above: Located in the heart of the restaurant, the stairway leading to the upper restaurant floor is flanked by mirror-lined walls that create spectacular, even humorous, perspectives.

Right: Behind a stone column, the central mirrored volume of the restaurant conceals the kitchen and produces almost-magical reflections.

a cultural fusion of senses

A magnet for countless painters, sculptors and designers from around the world, Ubud is the cultural centre of Bali. Local art forms—painting, stone and wood carving, silver work—still take place on a daily basis. It is therefore natural that this location in the Sayan district was chosen as the site for the Gaya "Fusion of Senses" Gallery. As one of the many initiatives launched in recent years to promote cultural and artistic exchange, the Gallery is an arts and cultural centre designed to develop and promote young local and foreign artists as well as to encourage international exchange. Run by two young, talented Italian designers, the Gallery already houses many world-class designs by contemporary designers and artists.

The two-storey building—in local wood and stone—is striking for its avant-garde, almost spaceship-like form (see left). Two ramp-like geometrical forms of *palimanan* stone and wood flank the oblong entrance in the middle. The unusual thatched roof that shelters the entire first floor is built in traditional *alang alang*. This top level is open on all four sides to allow full view of the beautiful surrounding countryside from the restaurant and bar. The ground floor is entirely given over to various design and painting exhibitions, as well as live cultural and musical performances.

Opposite: An unusual lamp in black bamboo and wood poses with a pencil drawing and a metal oil burner with a *palimanan* stone base.

Top: An old *dodot* cotton fabric from Solo in Java, dyed gold by the *batik* technique, forms a rich backdrop to a mix of furnishing accessories: two black bamboo lamps, a *palimanan* stone vase, and an assortment of cotton cushions.

Above: The living area, designed in a spare contemporary style, showcases the Italian designers' ideas in furnishings and interiors. The boxy design of the chunky rattan sofa is duplicated in the print of the cushions. In the foreground is an old mat from Borneo. A large portrait by Filippo Sciascia looks on.

Left: Inspired by local tradition, this oil and essence burner, made of iron and *palimanan* stone, is displayed together with a ceramic and coconut wood incense burner.

Above: At the back of the gallery, a wooden bridge over a narrow decorative pool leads to a small garden, heralded by a contemporary stone sculpture by Quarzia.

Above: The furnishings in this bedroom include a chair in coconut and teak wood, a 'fish trap' table lamp, and an oil on canvas by Filippo Sciascia.

Above: There is a very modernist feel of pared down lines in this bathroom, despite the spare furnishings, as the focus is on surfaces and textures. Against the white smoothness of the *palimanan* stone wall, a rustic bamboo ladder is decorated with beautiful silk sarongs. The black stone hanging vase, with its bold curves, is a special point of interest.

Left: A candle holder in wood and *palimanan* stone.

vibrant presentations

The Kayu-Kayu Gallery is the result of close collaboration between Balinese art lover Tri Susila and Italian architect Giovanni D'Ambrosio. The aim was not only to form an exhibition space for presenting beautiful works by contemporary Balinese artists but also to achieve an environment that is an exhibition in itself.

D'Ambrosio worked primarily with two sets of elements: slatted teak backdrops and geometric forms. In counterpoint to these features and poised within the contemporary arena, the black-painted floor-to-ceiling bamboo poles are a cultural reference to the ecology of the island. Both groups of components work together to set off the traditional art pieces—pliant Balinese sculptures and eye-catching Indonesian paintings—to the full. The finished gallery is a remarkable fusion of a skilfully designed modern setting and the intense sinuosity of the wooden Balinese artwork.

Above and left: A close-up look at two of many supple Balinese figures in the gallery.

Opposite: The visitor is immediately conscious, as he enters at the entrance, of a fantastic fusion of the modern setting of the place with the intense plasticity of the traditional Balinese figures created by the Indonesian artists. The blend of broken yellow and green stone pieces, in the floors, and white stone in the walls, creates an appealing contemporary backdrop for the sinuous pieces of supple wood art. Ahead, a big sculpture representing the Hindu deity, Dewi Ratih, by I Ketut Gelidih was carved from the root of a frangipani tree. Against the back wall is a painting of a mystic figure by Balinese painter I Made Djirna.

Right: Cleverly positioned black bamboo poles create attention-grabbing detail and set off the artworks on display. Against the slatted wooden back wall is a painting of three ladies (partially shown in the picture) by Nyoman Sukari (Karangsem, 1968), while on left is an amazing figure of a dancer by Balinese sculptor Mangku Wetja. The eye is then drawn to the two wall niches, which hold two small Wayan Pudja sculptures in *bentawas* wood, from Bali.

Below: A backdrop of multiple colours and contrasting shapes and textures grabs at the senses—spotted yellow of the wall in the foreground, warm brown of the slatted panel against the back, green of the stone used in the flooring, straw colour of the mat, and white of the stone walls. Taking centre stage is a sculpture by Balinese artist Wayan Subrata. In the foreground, the arching forms of a dancing figure by Balinese sculpture Mangku Wetja gives the viewer pause.

bali by design

"Glass Piano" sculpture in laminated glass and sandblasted glass keys on a stone base, by Seiki Torige.

Artistic collaboration between outsiders and the Balinese is no new phenomenon. The intense creativity of the local population, the glut of wonderful and plentiful natural materials, and the celebration of the Hindu Dharma long drawn foreign artists to the island. The result has been works of assimilation, exchange and adaptation, as well as new forms.

In recent years, many such collaborations have turned into highly profitable operations. The lure of a pleasant climate, a cheap and talented local workforce and an abundant choice of materials with which to work act as the magnet for artists, designers and craftspeople from as far afield as the US, Canada, Europe, Australia and other parts of Asia. The cottage industries and individual artists of the 20th century have transformed into 21st-century conglomerates. Large factories, mechanized (as well as made-by-hand) processes and modern materials are the physical manifestations of this new wave. Artistic influences from abroad are the impetus behind it.

Because of the island's unprecedented building boom, local demand is high for all types of decor items. Lavish interiors need modish decor accessories. This chapter presents a selection of up-to-the-minute furniture and furnishings, fabrics, kitchenware, tableware, lighting accessories, and garden features. There is also a selection of purely decorative objects—sculptures and paintings, for example—that will appeal to any tropical lifestyle afficionado. All items have that wonderful Bali-inspired feel—a feel-good factor any homemaker cherishes. As the originality and quality of such collections improve, export beckons. Nowadays, you are as likely to find them in overseas boutiques as in the local galleries and stores. Bali's mark in the tropical design world is assured.

freehand

1. A composition of a low table carved from an aged piece of *jati* wood (teakwood) with its four legs stained black; a chair made from one single piece of mahogany; and a standing lamp made of rice paper and mesh.

2. "Hokora": A unique standing lamp, carved from coconut wood, with an internal feature in recycled glass.

3. An altar piece, with ebony insertions, converted from an old mortar that was made out of one single block of wood.

4. Two stools made from *nangka* wood (jackfruit wood).

5. Two chairs in *nangka* wood, an African inspiration, and a stool in *jati* wood.

Sumio Suzuki's work has taken him to countless places—Asia, Africa, and North America—but the artist has finally settled in Ubud, Bali, a place which he sees as reminiscent of his native Japan. To Suzuki's mind, every piece has a purpose, and, through a trial-and-error process, the craftsmen he works with help provide an alternative view to his visions. "I draw the lines," he explains, "but the carvers inevitably produce mistakes as they give shape to my drawings, which grants me a different perspective of the original design." Suzuki's materials come from various species of large trees in Indonesia. The artist recognizes the characteristics of different types of wood and carefully applies their unique qualities to each piece. Suzuki's work reflects his philosophy about the "true nature of art": "My artwork should not reflect myself. Instead, it should transform itself to the life of its new owner."

shapes and textures

1. A long oval dish made of palm tree wood is an attractive receptacle for these tangerines.

2. A "mod-design with still life" composition against a *wonosari* ivory stone wall, comprising a wire-mesh and rice paper mixed media work by Sumio Suzuki; a console, stool and vase layered in striped dark coconut and penshell, and an oval pebble sculpture in crackled white coconut shell.

3. A square dish in striped coco shell with black penshell trim.

4. Two boxes made from striped white and dark coconut shell.

5. Various textures and finishings meet on top of this console, made of sliced white coconut shell. The lamp has a base in check-patterned stained green penshell, while the bowl is made out of striped white and dark coconut shell.

For Etienne de Souza, a visit to Bali some years ago unwittingly became a lifelong commitment. He was so intrigued by the wealth of artistic and cultural experience, he decided to turn to creating furniture and accessory collections from natural and exclusively local materials, including coconut fibre, palm tree wood, and mother-of-pearl and sea shells. His chosen media necessitate much planing, sanding and polishing—exacting tasks that de Souza derives much inspiration from. The French artist's secret lies in his intuitive knowledge that, in the creation of any object, time—and, by extension, patience—are the most important requisites, for they allow the material to communicate its essence to and inspire the artist. Only then, he believes, will the artwork be truly special.

2

circles and spirals

1. "Spiral", an 80-cm (31-in) natural hard-wood chiselled and sanded item, is simple yet most intriguing.

2. A garden composition of natural hardwood forms: "Spike", a 60-cm (24-in) sculpture in the foreground, resembles a huge seashell; on left is "Ridge", a 60-cm (24-in) piece; while closer up on right is "Pyramid", an 80-cm (31-in) artwork.

3. "Spikes", a pair of 60-cm (24-in) and 40-cm (16-in) natural hardwood decorative pieces in the shape of seashells, sits pretty at this landing.

4. "Seeds", 35-cm (14-in) display pieces made of natural hardwood, are perfect ornamentation for the top of a console.

5. This pair of 45-cm (18-in) natural hard-wood forms is called "Double Erosion".

6. "Space", a 105-cm (41-in) natural hard-wood piece, resembles a huge conch.

Dutch Carola Vooges's work reflects her deep love for tropical nature and her fascination with natural forms. But rather than merely reproducing these forms, she removes them from their usual contexts and recasts them using enhanced sizes and new textures, thus transforming them into sensual modern objects. Of her simple and natural style, Vooges explains: "My works belong to the tradition of Constantin Brancusi and Isamu Noguchi". A few years ago, she began her current series of sculptures, carving them out of either *suar* (a light fine-grained wood) or *waru* (a hardwood). All her art pieces are carved by hand, using traditional Balinese iron chisels, then sanded. The finish is natural and the resultant *objets* are brilliant and intriguing.

tribal contemporary

1. Giada works with everyday, traditional or vernacular elements, which she transforms into pieces of art. Here we have a recreation of an old wheat millstone.

2. A 'cuneum' console in recycled and glued teak. The vases on it are made of Javanese *palimanan* stone, while the picture backdrop is composed of Irian Jaya beads, by Produs Trend.

3. "The Big Anvil" in ironwood has a unique finish—the dye was achieved using a mix of petals and seeds from exotic fruits.

4. A mask from Borneo is mounted on an antique mortar as a decorative furnishing element. The coloured teak lamp is an African inspiration.

5. A huge ironwood bowl, carved by the Dayaks of Borneo, makes a solid impression.

6. This '60s-inspired console, hand-crafted from solid wood, is accompanied by a small anvil-shaped stool, an African inspiration. The key to the composition is ethnic minimalist.

Milanese designer Giada Barbieri draws inspiration not only from the compact force of tropical wood, but also from traditional objects. In the best tradition of abstract art, and in her search to represent its essence, Barbieri abandons superfluous detail when shaping the raw material. Imbued with a tribal strength, yet with their shape and volume in the style of contemporary minimalism, her pieces achieve a logically improbable yet successful fusion—the art of African and Bornean tribes and that of Romanian sculptor Constantin Brancusi. Barbieri accomplishes this remarkable complementarity of the characteristics of two worlds—old and modern—with the assistance of artisans from Java and Borneo.

the beauty of glass

1. Young coconut flowers decorate the "Giant Sushi Plate", a rippled pattern handmade glass platter.

2. A red, blue and white abstract painting by a Balinese artist serves as a dramatic backdrop for a free-form recycled glass sculpture, "Vessel", on a black console

3 & 5. A transparent hand-blown glass vase and a sandblasted hand-blown glass vase are perfect receptacles for tall plants, such as heliconias.

4. This recycled chiselled glass work with an unusual shape is quite aptly named "Boat".

6. A fully laminated glass bar counter at the Biji restaurant at Begawan Giri Estate, outside Ubud.

Drawn by the tactile beauty of glass, Seiki Torige, a master glass craftsman and designer, works recycled glass through all stages of production—melting, blowing, carving and sculpting. He often moulds the glass together with wood and iron, too. His impressive collection of modern glass designs range from flower vases to decorative tableware. At his recent debut Bali exhibition, Torige's words testify to his devotion to his chosen art form: "I met with numerous, unbelievable failures. Each failure felt as if part of me had died as such incredible effort had been poured into each creation. I came back to life as each success was achieved. All the pieces in the exhibition were the fruit of this experience. Anyone who comes to this exhibition shares both my failures and successes with me."

8

9

7. The "Lombardi chair" is an amazing mixed-media sculpture concocted from teakwood planks, recycled glass and metal.

8. "*Banyak Susu*", a slumped glass work laminated with sequin inserts. The dish in the foreground is "Elephant Foot", made of recycled glass.

9. The "fish logo", made of recycled slumped glass, and the custom made *sushi* and *sake* dinner set make a striking impression at Wasabi, a Japanese restaurant in Seminyak.

metalwork

1. This double-seater in stainless steel and leather has legs shaped like a *keris* (a ceremonial dagger). The shape of the chair is inspired by various *batik* patterns, while the mirror is in the shape of *dodot*, a traditional decorative shape.

2. This low table in stainless steel, with a Balinese lava stone top, is inspired by Middle Eastern calligraphy. The stainless steel lamp, with a base also made of lava stone, is inspired by "*parang rusak*", or a double helix. The polka-dotted lampshade is of Spandex.

3. Small table lamps, made of stainless steel, with a lava stone base and Thai silk shades.

4. Industrial chic table and chairs made of stainless steel, lava stone and leather.

5. This steel door with an oversized handle has a "*mega mendung*" ("cloudy sky") cut-out; the pattern is adapted from a Chinese design and is typically used in Javanese sarongs.

Indonesian sculptor Pintor Sirait's chosen art medium is metal. His work encompasses an impressive collection of commissioned practical and decorative applications, ranging from open-air monuments and wall sculptures to spiral staircases and table lamps. Sirait, who now lives in Bali, draws inspiration from various local myths and their relation to present human conditions. The artist always approaches each work with a strong intensity. In his recent pieces, he merges traditional Indonesian *batik* patterns with contemporary designs. The result is a collection of inspiring objects that not only reflect modern lifestyles and attitudes but are also reminiscent of traditional Bali.

flower mélange

1. Hand-painted blue leaf motif on an ivory cotton pillowcase. On top of it is blue organza.

2. A fine table cover made of organza silk with hand-painted floral motifs.

3. Red draperies of polyester and nylon form the backdrop for colourful silk pillows with hand-embroidered Laotian motifs.

4. Ivory cotton and natural fibre comprise this pillowcase of hand-painted floral motifs.

5. Hand-painted floral motifs adorn these organza silk pillow covers.

6. Organza silk pillowcases with hand-beaded floral motifs.

French fabric designer Dominique Seguin grew up along the Mekong river in Cambodia. As an adult she spent many years working for several fashion houses in Paris and elsewhere in Europe, then later moved back to a tropical country—this time it was to Bali.

Here, inspired by the renowned skills of the local artisans, she began developing her own designs in soft fabrics and furnishings. Her work experience in the fashion houses had sensitized her to the beauty of different materials and also endowed her with a sixth sense for the subtlety of colours. This is evident throughout her collections, which are made from organza, linen and silk. As she is inspired by the gentle, lush tropical nature of Bali, Seguin's refined designs often echo environmental subjects: delicate but vivid leaves, flowers and other plant motifs are created and produced by in-house embroiderers and painters.

crafted precision

1. This tiny container, skilfully concocted from coconut, silver and semi-precious stones, is playfully named "Joker", as it resembles a jester!

2. A teakwood writing desk with ebony inserts is accompanied by a movable multifunctional cabinet, made up of four hinged columns on wheels.

3. An innovatively designed relaxing chair in teakwood, teak plywood, copper and hand-woven fabric.

4. This narrow cabinet is crafted out of teak plywood and set on a *palimanan* ivory stone base.

5. A dining room sideboard made of *merbau* tropical wood and black lava stone. At centre, a table pendulum clock in teakwood, silver and coral pulp has strong deco lines.

In 1992, Giuseppe Verdacchi began designing and producing furniture and furnishing accessories in Bali. His creations are based on the goal of achieving a balance of volumes and also on defining the message an object should communicate within its context. Beppe, as the architect-designer is otherwise known, deliberately refrains from adhering to any one architectural school of thought. He goes about designing and producing his pieces in an extremely methodical way. Hence, the interaction between surfaces, the definition of their lines of contact, the way the different parts are conjoined, and the weights of the respective materials, are all extremely important considerations to him.

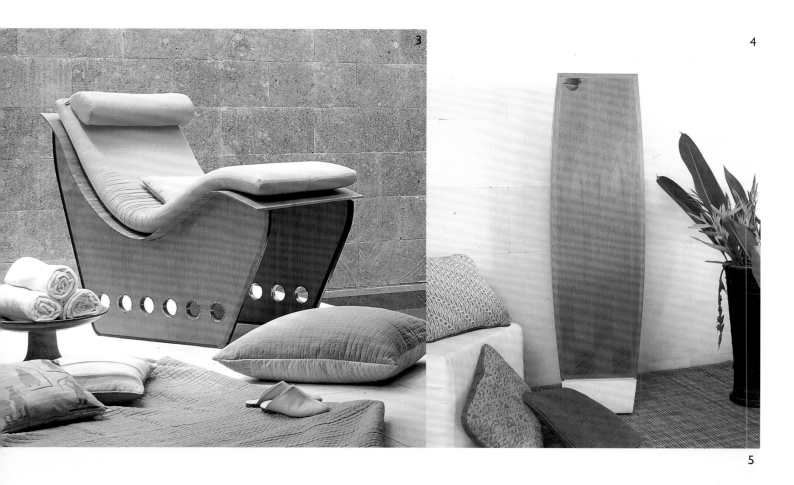

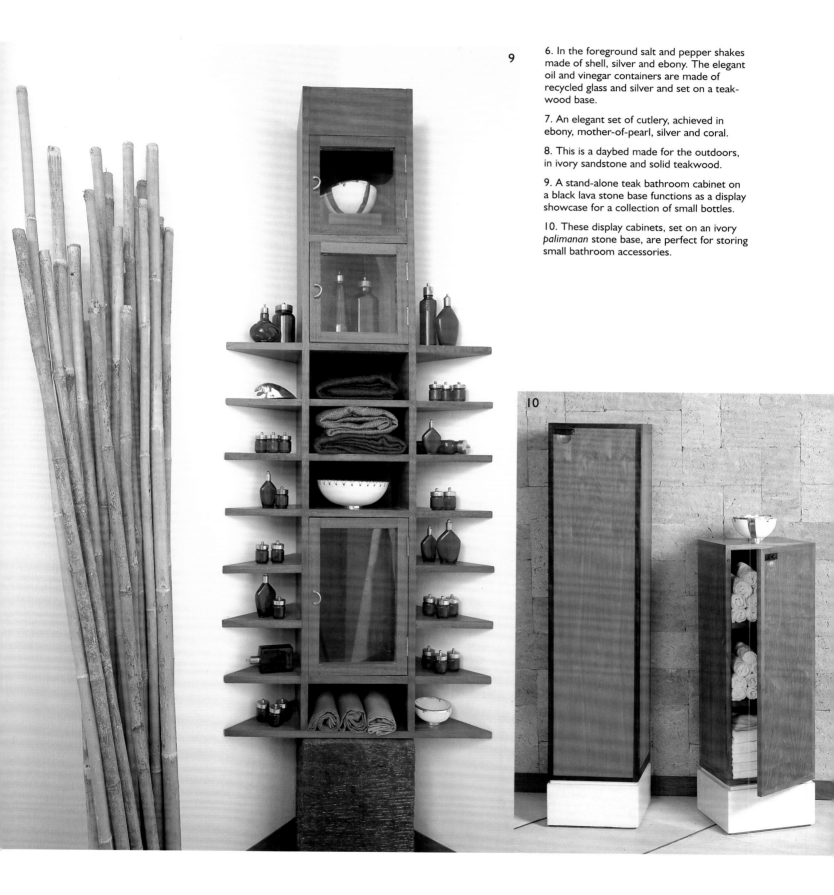

9

6. In the foreground salt and pepper shakes made of shell, silver and ebony. The elegant oil and vinegar containers are made of recycled glass and silver and set on a teakwood base.

7. An elegant set of cutlery, achieved in ebony, mother-of-pearl, silver and coral.

8. This is a daybed made for the outdoors, in ivory sandstone and solid teakwood.

9. A stand-alone teak bathroom cabinet on a black lava stone base functions as a display showcase for a collection of small bottles.

10. These display cabinets, set on an ivory *palimanan* stone base, are perfect for storing small bathroom accessories.

10

trendy tropical

1. Plates, handmade in polished square-patterned white bone.

2. "Mango Line": a console made of teakwood stained a dark mahogany, with white bone inlays, is composed here with a polished bone vase, a wood and polished bone fruit cup, and a decorative wall panel in dark stained wood.

3. "Jungle" tray, made of bamboo pieces and red and black resin framed by dark stained wood.

4. Trays in polished white bone.

5. "Astek" tray in curved patterned pieces of bamboo and black resin.

6. A table lamp base made of white polished bone spheres on wood.

7. "Cube": A table lamp in a black and white check pattern made of white bone and black penshell.

8. A rectangular centre-table display: a sushi tray in bamboo and black resin with decorative fruit in white polished bone.

Produs Trend was set up by Italian Roberto Tenace and French architect Meriem Hall for experimenting with forms and materials for interior design. The two artists design and produce unique collections using different organic materials, such as wood, bone and shell, together with fabrics, resin and metals. Tenace enjoys harnessing different arts and crafts techniques in producing furnishing accessories that are imbued with the aesthetic temperament and style of his native country. Hall, on the other hand, has a firmly entrenched vision of merging the cultural and artistic heritage of Paris and Bali in the furniture pieces. The artistic production of these two individuals is, without fail, refreshing and thought provoking.

radiant lights

1. "Yoyo", a simple rectangular table lamp, with a home-produced moulded glass diffuser and a central element in laminated glass, which has a reflecting and aesthetic purpose.

2. A large "Rayo" halogen standing lamp with clean refined lines and art deco influences.

3. These small "Diago" lamps on a wooden base can be totally disassembled. They are made of two tensioned stripes of wood curved and mortised together.

4. The "Pyramid" table lamp has a white and green cone-shaped diffuser, made out of a pyramidal homemade blow mould.

5. This collection, "Sequence", comprises table lamps in different shapes and sizes. They are of a wooden structure, and combined with laminated glass, which acts as the diffuser. The artist fondly labels them "Modern Asiatique".

Based in Bali since 1998, Marc Le has nurtured his passion for wood since a young age. He began his artistic career by teaching himself the exacting craft of cabinet making, and then became an antique-cabinet restorer. Much later, he started to design cabinets and other one-off wooden furniture pieces before finally turning his creative skills to lighting accessories. Today the artist owns a company, aptly named Radiant, and he almost exclusively designs and creates lights and lighting designs. Working with the remarkably ductile yet resilient local *merbau* or ironwood, and glass, he takes the classic lamp to new heights. Finding inspiration in contemporary sculpture as well as in art deco, Marc Le's collections are versatile, sensitive and subtle.

delighting ideas

1. Looking at home in a tropical setting, this "Kalimantan" table lamp has an antique traditional pattern; its pyramid shaped base is made of woven Borneo rattan.

2. "Natural Element" standing lamp on stone base, made out of bamboo with a natural finish, bound with coconut rope and combined with a light coloured silk diffuser.

3. "Mirage" table lamp, with a black lacquered wooden rectangular base and a diffuser comprised of aluminium rods.

4. This "Ali Baba" table lamp has a hammered aluminium base etched with a "water drops" effect.

5. "Sucre", a collection of wooden standing and table lamps with bottle-shape bases of coconut wood and black and white wash finishing. The diffuser is made of *kampil* (a material used for packing rice).

6. The "Artu" table lamp is composed with a brass crown bronze finish with a stamped motif; its sculptured diffuser is constructed of aluminium mesh.

British-born Sue Kilmister has a Law degree, but she chose instead to devote her life to art and design. In the nineties she researched geometric alabaster lights, geomantic design and postmodern Chinese style, and produced several collections of decorative lighting, both in Italy and in USA. Kilmister later merged her style with that of Carlo Forzinetti, with whom she set up a company. The latter is particularly intrigued by vernacular traditions, the use of the materials and signs, and sculpture and design. Based in Bali and supported by a crew of skilled artisans, their company produces lighting collections, created from a variety of materials and forms harnessing the artistic eclecticism and creative backgrounds of its owners.

2

1. A table lamp with a diffuser made from the fibre of pineapple, with a black gloss glazed ceramic base.

2. Table lamp duo: The one featured on the left has a large egg-shaped base with a white matt glaze and a shell motif print; its diffuser is realized in black and white *plissé*. The smaller lamp on right has a stone base with different glazed surfaces—white sandblasted on the bottom, black speckled gloss on the top—and a silk diffuser.

3. A company of table lamps with various coloured ceramic bases, realized with a crackled aesthetic finish with silk diffuser.

4. Table lamps with ceramic bases that are inspired by *mamuli*, a traditional gold pendant from Sumba island; the diffuser is of silk.

5. Table lamps with ceramic bases with different glosses and textured with a cotton *bouclé* diffuser.

Kilmister and Forzinetti also collaborate with Bali's premier ceramic company, Jenggala Keramik, to jointly design and produce unusual lamp designs. Having created ceramic items, tableware and table top accessories for more than twenty years, Jenggala has evolved from a small experimental cottage industry to a manufacturer of high quality handmade products. Inspired by the technological expertise, the natural materials and the wide range of shapes and glaze finishes available from Jenggala, the two designers have created several unique lighting objects, some of which are displayed on these pages.

ethnic modernity

1. This "Zen" standing lamp has been specially designed for big spaces, such as in restaurants or a hotel lobby. It is formed by stacking two different sized cylinders, in raw silk, one on top of the other; both are light diffusing.

2. A real example of ethnic modern design, this standing lamp rests on a simple bamboo ladder base. The lamp shade is made of two rectangular diffusers in resin fabric.

3. The "Lamu" table lamp has a base that comprises a lacquered wood rectangular frame and a dyed leaf insert; the coloured lampshade is made of cotton.

4. This multifunctional designed lamp is made of resin fabric framed in dark brown stained wood. It can be used as a wall, hanging, or table lamp.

By combining the use of ethnic materials with modern, sleek shapes, and by paying careful attention to technical details and the choice of materials, Claire Guillot and Ken Vigoni, whose company is Piment Rogue, design and produce very original lighting accessories, ranging from table and floor lamps, to wall lights, hanging lights and chandeliers. The shape and form of the material—wood is their favourite—is enhanced through decorative effects such as shells, and Asian figurines, or by the use of organic elements such as coconut shell and bamboo. Deep red lacquers are then applied to yield a bold and modern finish. These lamps and lights are true works of art.

Acknowledgements

Credits

p32: Rustic colonial table in teakwood by Warisan; white ceramic dinner ware by Palanquin; glasses made of recycled glass by Seiki Torige.

pp36-37: Small black and white paintings (on the wall) by Jim Elliot, modern portrait by Filippo Sciascia; flat red cushion and three pillows by The Grotto; blue glass vases by Seiki Torige; black console (centre right) by Esok Lusa; coffee table (foreground) by Dean Kempnich; table lamp in wood and glass by Marc Le; sofa upholstery, fabrics, Japanese *tatami* and pillows by Martina Urbas.

p39: Dining table and console by Dean Kempnich; black painting on the wall by Made Bendesa; chairs by Esok Lusa.

p42: Chinese chest and colonial coffee table (on left) by Warisan; old Pakistani carpet (on right) by Dominique Seguin; rectangular table lamp by Palanquin.

p44: Dining table designed by Dean Kempnich; chairs from Esok Lusa.

p45: Hand-printed Indian cotton pillows and bed cover, Pakistani antique camel bag and *kilim* by Dominique Seguin.

p47: "The Giant Flip Flip" standing lamp with silk shade by Delighting; fabrics for pillows and mattress by Quarzia for Gaya Design.

p49: Figurative painting by Filippo Sciascia; "Bamboo T" table lamp (in the corner) by Delighting for Jenggala Keramik; "Mango Line" wooden coffee tables with bone inlay designed by Meriem Hall for Produs Trend; grey stone sculpture on left by Dutch sculptor Reinko; fabrics and pillows by Quarzia for Gaya Design; white ceramic accessories on the coffee table by Gaya Ceramic; book holder with terracotta heads (foreground) by Produs Trend.

p50: Paintings by Filippo Sciascia; "Mango Line" black wooden console with bones inlay and stainless steel rods designed by Meriem Hall for Produs Trend; two white stone sculptures (on the console) by Reinko; black bamboo lamp (right corner) by Gaya Design.

p111: Red and green drapes in organza and silk, as well as upholstery and table lampshades, all in silk, designed by Dominique Seguin.

p126: Chairs by Giovanni D'Ambrosio; console on left by Meriem Hall for Produs Trend; bamboo table lamp on the console with silk shade; standing lamp in black wood and silk shade (background) by Delighting.

p127 (above): "The Fifth Element" standing lamp in bamboo and woven silk shade by Delighting.

p127 (right): Sofa and coffee table (foreground) by Produs Trend; "Quadripod" standing lamp (on right) in black lacquered wood and silk *plissé* shade by Delighting.

p135: Table lamp (background) in stained green penshell by Etienne De Souza; "Pebbles" in white coco and dark penshell (foreground) and armchair (on right) in striped coco shell by Etienne De Souza.

p138: "Sucre", a collection of standing and table lamps in black and white washed finish coconut wood by Delighting; chairs in dark coco finish by Kasmil Kosmos; shaped pie unit and top of dining table by Etienne de Souza.

pp150–155: All the furnishings and the accessories shown in "A Cultural Fusion of Senses" are by Gaya Design. The paintings are by Filippo Sciascia.

p192: Dinner set in metal and black ceramic by Marilena Vlataki.

References

Giada Barbieri
jada.b@tiscalinet.it

Giovanni D'Ambrosio
vanbergen_dambrosio@hotmail.com

Gaya Design
gaya@gayafusion.com
Gaya Gallery, Jl. Raya Sayan, Ubud

Delighting
Jl. Gatot Subroto 99, Kerobokan

Esok Lusa
Jl. Raya Basangkasa 47, Seminyak
gundul@eksadata.com

GM
gmarc@tiscalinet.it

Joost van Grieken
joost@idola.net.id

Claire Guillot / Ken Vigoni
piment_rouge@lycos.com
Susuk, Jl. Raya Kerobokan 35, Kuta

Meriem Hall
mhall@club-internet.fr

Sue Kilmister / Carlo Forzinetti
delight@indosat.net.id

Marc Le
marcle@dps.centrin.net.id
Radiant, Jl. Raya Seminyak #4A, Basangkasa

Dean Kempnich
deank91@hotmail.com

David Lombardi
dave@fullondesign.com

Palanquin
info@palanquinbali.com
Jl. By Pass Ngurah Rai 8, Simpang Siur, Kuta

Quarzia
gaya@gayafusion.com

Dominique Seguin
disini_bali@yahoo.com
Disini, Jl. Raya Seminyak 68, Basangkasa

Filippo Sciascia
gaya@gayafusion.com

Pintor Sirait
sculpt@indo.net.id
info@liludesign.com

Etienne de Souza
etienne@idola.net.id

Sumio Suzuki
sumio@indo.net.id

Roberto Tenace
trend777@indosat.net.id

Seiki Torige
gundul@eksadata.com

Martina Urbas
martina@archipelonline.com

Giuseppe Verdacchi
verdachi@indosat.net.id

Marilena Vlataki
www.bali-marilena.com
Selini, Jalan Dyana Pura 5, Seminyak

Carola Vooges
carolavogue@aol.com

Anneke van Waesberghe
esp2000@indo.net.id
www.espritnomade.net

Warisan
warisan@indosat.net.id

Note from the Author

I would like to extend my gratitude to all the people who allowed us into their houses for the photography and to all artists featured in the book.
Thanks to Maggy Greenhorn for her important contributions to the literary aspects of the book.
Thanks to Kim Inglis for her highly professional and precious support.
A special thank you to editor Jocelyn Lau for her continuous and patient support in every stage of the layout and compilation of the book.
And as usual it was a pleasure to work with my good friend Luca.